MATT CHRISTOPHER®

On the Court with...

MATT CHRISTOPHER®

On the Court with...

Yao Ming

Text by Glenn Stout

LITTLE, BROWN AND COMPANY
New York ·· Boston

Little, Brown and Company

Time Warner Book Group
1271 Avenue of the Americas, New York, NY 10020
Visit our Web site at www.lb-kids.com

First Edition

Matt Christopher® is a registered trademark of Catherine M. Christopher.

Cover photograph by John W. McDonough / Sports Illustrated
© Time Inc.

Library of Congress Cataloging-in-Publication Data

Stout, Glenn, 1958–
    On the court with — Yao Ming / [text written by Glenn Stout].
    — 1st ed.
        p. cm.
    At head of title: Matt Christopher.
    ISBN: 0-316-73574-4
    1. Ming, Yao, 1980– — Juvenile literature.   2. Basketball players —
China — Biography — Juvenile literature.   I. Christopher, Matt.
II. Title.

GV884.M558S86 2004
796.323'092 — dc22

                                                        2004001410

10 9 8 7 6 5 4 3 2 1

COM-MO

Printed in the United States of America

Contents

Chapter One: 1980–1994   1
The Next Big Thing

Chapter Two: 1994–1996   14
The Universal Game

Chapter Three: 1996–1999   22
First Steps to the NBA

Chapter Four: 2000–2001   31
Hopeful Olympian

Chapter Five: 2001–2002   39
The Chinese Rocket

Chapter Six: 2002   50
Starting Slow

Chapter Seven: 2002   59
Growing Pains

Chapter Eight: 2002   66
Living in America

Chapter Nine: 2002   70
Coming Up Big

Chapter Ten: 2002–2003   79
Yao versus Shaq

Chapter Eleven: 2003   90
Worldwide All-Star

MATT CHRISTOPHER®

On the Court with...

Yao Ming

Chapter One:
1980–1994

The Next Big Thing

In December 1891, Dr. James Naismith, a physical-education teacher in Springfield, Massachusetts, invented the sport of basketball. Naismith hoped that the game would help keep his students fit throughout the long, cold winter. He succeeded beyond his wildest dreams. Basketball has since spread to virtually every nation on the face of the earth. It is one of the most popular sports in the world. People who speak different languages and grow up in different cultures have discovered that they can all come together on a basketball court.

In recent years, the National Basketball Association (NBA) has attracted the best players in the world, including Dallas Mavericks star forward Dirk Nowitski of Germany, New Jersey Nets center Dikembe Mutombo of the Democratic Republic of

Congo, and San Antonio Spurs guard Tony Parker of France. Basketball fans worldwide can watch their favorites players on television.

But one foreign player in the NBA literally stands above the rest. Houston Rockets center Yao Ming of China is perhaps the most popular basketball player in the world. Standing seven feet five inches, he is certainly one of the tallest. Fans everywhere thrill to his playing style and his pleasant and open personality. They love the fact that he can not only reach high above the rim to block a shot or throw down a thunderous dunk, but also that he can run the court on the fast break, block shots, throw a delicate "no look" pass to a teammate, or step back and shoot a soft jump shot.

After only one season in the NBA, Yao Ming is already on track to become one of the game's greatest players. As one sportswriter wrote, "Ming is not only the next big thing in basketball, he is the next *best* thing." In many people's opinion, Ming's skills and charisma can help the game of basketball grow, just as the great Michael Jordan's talent and appeal did.

Yet only a few decades ago, the notion of a Chinese basketball player appearing in the NBA or being one of the best players in the world would have seemed absurd. The game itself was barely known in China, and the few Chinese athletes who did play were hardly NBA caliber.

China has a long and fascinating history. For centuries, the nation has been isolated from the rest of the world by geography, culture, and language. Yet time after time, China was invaded by foreigners. As a result, China has often been distrustful of outsiders.

In 1949, a socialist government took over and created the modern Chinese nation, the People's Republic of China. The Chinese socialist government believes that for the common good of the people, it should control most facets of life — including the playing of sports.

For years, the Chinese government didn't consider sports to be very important for most of its citizens. Until recently, despite a population of more than 1.3 billion people (nearly five times the population of the United States), only a handful of Chinese citizens played basketball. The government recruited the few who did for a single purpose: to support the Chinese national team and participate in international competitions like the Olympic Games. Talented athletic children were selected by the government to attend special schools and sports academies so that they could learn to play the game in order to serve their country. Very few people just played the game for fun, and public basketball courts in China were rare.

But in the past couple of decades, that has changed. The government realized that exercise helps keep people strong and healthy, so it began encouraging citizens to play sports. Because playing basketball requires very little space and equipment, it became one of the more popular sports.

Starting in the early 1970s, China began to open its doors wider to foreign cultures. A way that these cultures reached China was through television, and sporting events are just one kind of program now seen on Chinese TV. When Chinese citizens began watching American basketball, they became more excited about the game.

Today, Chinese citizens have access to the Internet and select television programs from around the world, including NBA basketball games. Basketball has become very popular, particularly among younger people who live in big cities. Now perhaps as many as 200 million Chinese citizens play basketball. The country even has its own professional league, the Chinese Basketball Association (CBA). Regular-season CBA games are watched by as many as 130 million fans — more than the number of people who watch the Super Bowl in the United States!

It is no surprise, then, that Chinese basketball players have improved rapidly. Yao Ming may be the first great Chinese player, but it is unlikely that he will be the last.

Yao was born on September 12, 1980, the only child of Yao Zhi Yuan, his father, and Fang Feng Di, his mother. Although he is known here by the name "Yao," in China, a person's first name actually appears last. (For example, John Smith would be Smith John in China.) When his parents named their son Ming, his name became Yao Ming.

Yao grew up outside the large city of Shanghai. He began playing organized basketball when he was nine years old. By that age, he already knew how to dribble the ball and shoot, thanks in large part to his parents.

Yao's father and mother were Chinese basketball pioneers. His father is six feet seven, and his mother is six feet three. In the 1970s, both played for the Chinese national teams and competed in the Olympics. They met through playing basketball, and the game has always been an important part of their lives.

From the time that Yao could walk, there was always a basketball in the family's apartment. He liked nothing better than bouncing the ball back and forth. Growing up in a basketball family made dribbling and shooting almost second nature to him. But Yao's parents didn't force their son to play basketball. Like children in the United States, he was encouraged to have fun with other kids his age.

Yet even as a young boy, Yao stood out. He towered over his peers, and his skill with a ball was far beyond that of anyone else his age. When Yao was old enough, he joined a youth basketball league. There, his coaches quickly took note of his aptitude for the game.

Sports are very organized in China. The best players in a league are rapidly promoted to a better league. The Chinese try to identify the players with the most potential while they are still children and then arrange for them to receive special instruction.

At the age of twelve, Yao was selected to attend a special provincial sports academy in Shanghai called the Shanghai Physical and Sports Technic Education Institute, a private school for the best young athletes in the Shanghai area. Yao left home and went to live in a dormitory with other students.

Yao was a little frightened to be living away from home, although he saw his parents during vacations and other visits. But he also knew that attending the academy was a rare opportunity. And in the People's Republic of China, most citizens have to attend the schools that the government wants them to attend and do the kind of work that the government wants them to do. In exchange, the government provides housing, health care, and the other necessities of life. The government still controls most aspects of daily life, but it has somewhat relaxed its grip in recent years, and the Chinese have more freedom of choice now than in the past.

The best athletes are treated differently. The government wants China to do well at international competitions, so star athletes receive privileges that are not available to ordinary citizens. If a player is fortunate enough to become a member of the national team, he or she not only attends special schools, but also is paid a salary larger than that of most Chinese; is given a larger apartment; and enjoys additional perks, such as access to special stores stocked with food and other items unavailable to ordinary citizens. Both of Yao's parents had received such treatment when they were athletes. Yao knew that attending the academy could give him a chance to live a better life.

All of a sudden, Yao had to get serious about his future. He had to study hard at school and on the basketball court. The academy was very competitive, and Yao knew that if he didn't work hard, there were thousands of other young men in China who would love to take his place. Fortunately, he loved basketball. Unlike many of his classmates who quickly tired of the practices, training, and game-playing, Yao couldn't get enough of the sport.

His hard work paid off. At age fourteen, while still at the academy, he was selected to play center for the Shanghai Youth Team. Being part of this team was his first step toward becoming a member of the Chinese national team.

By this time, fourteen-year-old Yao stood close to six feet five — an unusual height in many countries, but even more so in China, where the average male height was approximately five feet five. Doctors monitoring the health of academy students were curious about how tall Yao would become. One way that doctors determine how much a young person will grow is by examining his or her knuckles. After measuring the knuckles of thousands of young athletes and then tracking their growth, Chinese doctors have learned to predict how much a young person will grow with remarkable accuracy.

When doctors measured Yao's knuckles, they were stunned. According to their calculations, Yao had a *lot* of growing to do. They calculated that as an adult, he would stand nearly seven and a half feet tall! Although there were many other players in the national basketball-development system who were more than seven feet tall, and some other young players expected to grow to this size, few had Yao's basketball skills and love of the game.

Yao was also fortunate that the Chinese basketball

federation was beginning to change and adapt to outside influences. For years, it had tried to produce players like a factory, forcing everyone to play the game the same way. As a result, although the best Chinese players were fundamentally sound in such game basics as shooting and dribbling, they didn't know how to adapt to the way that the game was played outside China. In most other countries, teams played an up-tempo style of basketball that they learned from watching the NBA. In contrast, the Chinese played slowly and predictably. But beginning in the 1980s, new technology — such as videotape and satellite television broadcasts — exposed Chinese players and coaches to the NBA style of play.

Yao, his friends, and his coaches at the academy now had the opportunity to watch how the game was played in the NBA. They were amazed by the level of skill that they saw, how fast the players ran, and how high they jumped. They learned all about Michael Jordan, whom they called "Qiao Dan," a Chinese name that not only sounds similar to "Jordan," but also is a term of respect that means skillful, strong, and clever. In addition, Yao enjoyed watching the Houston Rockets' Nigerian center, Hakeem Olajuwon, and Boston Celtics star Larry Bird. Yao could see that Bird, a remarkable passer, was responsible for creating, as Yao put it, "a new era of history." Little did he know that someday he would have the same opportunity to make basketball history.

Yao soaked up basketball like a sponge. On most days, he spent *four hours* either playing basketball or practicing basketball-related drills. Although his coaches wanted him to stay underneath the basket, block shots, rebound, and shoot lay-ups like a traditional center, Yao knew from watching the NBA that he had to do much more than just stand by the rim and wait for the ball.

Practical experience taught him the same thing. In most games, he was already being guarded by two or three players. His teammates often had a difficult time getting the ball to him. He realized that if he didn't learn how to move to create plays, he would never be more than just the tall guy who stood under the basket.

So Yao decided that he would learn to play the game like a player who was of average size. Whenever he had a free moment, he worked on his ball handling, passing, and jump shot. As his skills improved, his teammates began to realize that Yao was much more than a person who played basketball just because he was tall: he was a basketball player who just happened to be tall.

Although Yao's coaches were sometimes frustrated because he wouldn't always follow their instructions and stay under the basket, it was hard to argue with the results. He was a good shooter, and when he was covered, he knew how to pass the ball to an open teammate. Yao was becoming a rare kind of player — the kind who makes his teammates better. It was apparent that if he continued to play as well as he did, he would one day become a member of the national team.

Only a few years before, playing for the national team and appearing in the Olympics representing his or her country would have been the greatest dream that Yao or any other Chinese basketball player would dare dream. But ever so slowly, Yao and his countrymen were beginning to have dreams that extended beyond the borders of China. Although they never admitted it aloud, when Yao and his friends closed their eyes at night and dreamed about playing basketball, their dreams did not end with playing for China in the Olympics. They saw themselves playing with and against Michael Jordan, Hakeem Olajuwon, and other stars in the National Basketball Association.

Chapter Two:
1994-1996

The Universal Game

The NBA, or National Basketball Association, has been in existence since 1949. For much of its early history, nearly every player was an American, mainly because the sport had not yet spread throughout the world. But by the late 1960s, professional leagues had sprouted up in several European countries, and the game of basketball was being played all over the world.

Still, few foreign teams could compete on the same level as the best American squads. But by the early 1970s, this began to change. Socialist countries like the Soviet Union and East Germany took sports, particularly the Olympic Games, very seriously. They started sports academies and began training players at a young age. The Chinese government adopted a similar model.

While international play improved, American basketball fans believed that it would be decades before players from other countries could compete with the United States. But all that changed during the 1972 Olympics in Munich, West Germany. In the gold medal game, the Soviet Union defeated the United States basketball team. It was the first time that an American team had ever lost a basketball game in the Olympics. American fans were shocked.

The Soviet win gave international basketball a shot in the arm. At the same time, it shook up American basketball in two ways. First, the United States redoubled its efforts in Olympic basketball to try to prevent another defeat. And second, American coaches began looking at foreign players in a new light. The defeat opened their eyes to the possibility that players from other countries could be just as talented as their American counterparts. After all, no matter what language a player spoke, the ball was still the same size, and the hoop was still ten feet off the ground.

An informal international basketball-exchange program began to take place at the college level. American college coaches, eager to get the best players, started scouting other countries for players. At the same time, some foreign basketball organizations began steering select players to colleges in the United States. They realized that by playing against better competition, those athletes would improve. Then they could return and teach their countrymen the style of basketball that they had learned in the United States.

At the professional level, such exchanges were a bit more one-sided. While few non-Americans made it into the NBA, some Americans who didn't have enough talent to play for the NBA found spots on professional teams overseas. Others coached these same teams, which were often made up of players from more than one country.

As a result, the talent gap between foreign and American players narrowed through the 1970s and 1980s. By 1984, the NBA was taking a serious look at foreign players. In that year's draft, the New Jersey Nets selected sharp-shooting Brazilian guard Oscar Schmidt, who was a star in the Italian professional league. Schmidt was honored by the selection, but he chose to remain a star in Italy rather than risk riding the bench in the United States.

One year later, the Phoenix Suns drafted Georgi

Glouchkov, a center from Bulgaria. Although Glouchkov only played one season with limited success for the Suns, he proved that foreign players could contribute in the NBA. In every season since then, NBA teams have drafted more and more foreign players, and many have become stars.

But acquiring rights to foreign players is not always easy. The NBA has to convince the players' governments and sports associations to allow them to come to the United States to play. In many countries, a player's career is controlled by his country's national basketball federation to ensure that the individual continues to play for the national team. Without permission from the federation, an athlete can be legally stopped from playing professional basketball in the United States. In the 1980s and early 1990s, many foreign stars weren't allowed to play professionally in the United States until their best years as athletes were over. Only then were they allowed to play in the NBA. Nevertheless, in each season, more and more players from nations like Russia, Lithuania, Croatia, Nigeria, and the Sudan made it in the NBA. But there was one notable exception: China.

China wasn't eager to send players to the United

States to shoot hoops. As a socialist country, Chinese society values group achievement more than personal accomplishments. Into the 1990s, the only goal of its national basketball program was to provide players for the national team. Athletes who wanted to play in the United States were considered selfish.

At the same time, few Chinese players seemed likely candidates for the NBA. Despite the huge number of players in China and the growing influence of the NBA, the Chinese basketball program couldn't compete against the best teams in the world. They still played an old-fashioned style of basketball that wasn't very effective when they competed internationally. The Chinese didn't use the fast break very often. Every time they got the ball, they plodded down the court and set up the same few plays.

Many Chinese players were becoming frustrated by that style: they believed that their skills were being wasted. They wanted to play basketball the way that they saw it played on television by the NBA, but they knew that they wouldn't be able to do so until they had an opportunity to learn that style on the court, going up against better competitors.

Guard Ma Jian was the first notable Chinese player

to come to the United States. In 1988, Jian, at six feet seven, was already one of the best guards in China. Representatives of UCLA, an American college with a tremendous basketball program, saw Jian play in an international tournament and offered him a scholarship to attend their school and play for their team. But when Jian asked the government for permission to accept the offer, promising to return to China to play for the national team in the Olympics and in other big international competitions, Chinese authorities turned him down.

But Jian didn't stop asking. Finally, in 1992, the government allowed him to go to the United States. By that time, however, UCLA had withdrawn its scholarship offer. So Jian attended a junior college for one year and then transferred to the University of Utah. He played well enough that in 1995 and 1996 he tried out for the NBA. Both times, he was the last player cut in training camp by the Los Angeles Clippers. Jian was disappointed, but he had proven that a Chinese player could stand with some of the best players in the world.

Jian's near-miss in the NBA sparked some controversy in his home country. The national basketball federation considered Jian something of a traitor for going to the United States and had banned him from the national team in 1992. Yet when he returned to China in 1996, it was clear that he had improved much more rapidly than he would have had he remained in China. Jian could dribble between his legs and make passes behind his back just like American stars. He made most other Chinese players seem slow. One Chinese sportswriter admitted that the sports federation "hates him, but the sportswriters all like him because he has so much personality." The fans liked him, too. Jian wasn't afraid to criticize Chinese basketball, which he though was too regimented. "You have to do something different to be a success," he said.

Fortunately for Jian and other up-and-coming Chinese basketball players, "something different" was just what was happening to the game in China at that time. In 1995, the sports federation created the Chinese Basketball Association. Made up of a dozen teams, the CBA was formed with an eye to bettering China's basketball standings internationally. Association officials even allowed a handful of foreigners — some of them American — to play in the league.

Having seen how much Jian had improved after going to the United States, they understood that if Chinese basketball were to grow, athletes would have to learn to play basketball the way that it was played in the United States.

All this took place at the perfect time for Yao Ming. Just as he was reaching the top level of Chinese basketball, Chinese basketball was reaching out to the world.

Chapter Three:
1996–1999

First Steps to the NBA

As a teenager, Yao Ming was recognized by Chinese basketball officials as its future star. In 1997, he was named to the Chinese Under-22 national team and competed for his country in the Under-22 World Championships. One year later, at age seventeen, he came to the attention of Nike, the sporting-goods company.

Nike sponsored the Shanghai Sharks, one of the CBA's teams. Yao was signed up to play for the team during the 1997–98 season. But before the season started, Nike invited him to its All-American Camp, which was held in Paris in the summer of 1997. The camp was attended by young players from around the globe as well as by coaches and scouts from professional teams. Yao made the best of his time there, playing well enough to be noticed by such basketball notables as Del Harris, then coach of the Los Angeles Lakers.

Paris was just the first international stop of Yao's summer. From there he traveled with his fellow Shark, Liu Wei, to Indianapolis, Indiana, where he joined 200 top young American ballplayers for another All-American Camp.

Many college coaches scout the camp in search of players. When Yao arrived, few American coaches had ever heard of him. The few who had expected him to be slow and uncoordinated. No one thought that he could hold his own against the best high-school players in America.

But by the end of camp, Yao was all everyone was talking about. He had done much more than hold his own. Camp organizers ranked him second out of 40 centers at the camp. Although his skills were still raw, and he weighed only about 225 pounds, observers had never seen a player so simultaneously tall and talented. Yao was in control of his body, and his movements were smooth and sure. He could shoot jump shots with the control of smaller players and was one of the best passing larger players in camp. Even though stronger players easily pushed him around, at seven feet five, Yao knew how to use his height and blocked his share of shots. And when a player pushed Yao too hard, he pushed back. As one American player described him, "He's got the ability to run up and down the court, has a nice touch, good basic skills. Combine that with being seven feet five, and you've got tremendous potential." His performance at the camp was so impressive that he earned the ranking of second-best center.

Yao also earned the chance to be a counselor at Michael Jordan's Flight School in Santa Barbara, California. Suddenly, the seventeen-year-old was about to come face to face with Michael Jordan, or "Qiao Dan," the best player in the world.

The Flight School is a basketball training camp for boys and girls ages 8 through 18. Coaches and players teach the youngsters the basics of the game: dribbling, shooting, passing, and more. Although Yao could speak very little English, he managed to fit in without a problem as a counselor. And best of all, he got to play with and against Michael Jordan and other star players in nightly five-on-five scrimmages. In one memorable game, Jordan drained a three-pointer, then challenged Yao to try to do the same. Yao sank it without a problem. Jordan's comment? "Wow, the big guy can shoot!"

Almost overnight, Yao Ming had become the buzz of United States basketball. Nearly every college-basketball program in the country wanted him to play for them. But Yao simply wasn't available.

The Chinese had no intention of sending him to play college basketball in the United States. The national team needed him. It wanted Yao to play with its other big men, seven-foot Menk Bateer and seven foot, one-inch Wang Zhizhi, and to prepare for the 2000 Olympics. At the same time, Yao's emerging talents were needed for the Chinese Basketball Association's Shanghai Sharks.

When Yao returned to China for the start of the 1997–98 season as a member of the Shanghai Sharks, his skills had improved, thanks in part to his exposure to the game in America. He had also grown physically — to a height of more than seven feet. However, his upper-body strength was very slight and, as a result, he got knocked around a lot during his rookie year. Still, he managed to average 10 points and 8.3 rebounds a game that season.

Yao's 1998–99 season was cut short when he broke his leg. In the twelve games he played, however, he more than doubled his game-point average to 20.9. The next season, he was back in top form, playing 33 games and racking up a total of 699 points and 480 rebounds. In addition, he reached the pinnacle of Chinese basketball when he was named to the National Team.

His rapid progress, great size, and skill made him the talk of the Chinese basketball community. And coaches and scouts from the United States hadn't forgotten him, either.

However, China had no intention of letting their big man go. For one thing, Yao's presence had increased attendance at CBA games. Attendance and television ratings were just as important to the CBA as they were to the NBA. Yao was seen as vital to the health of the league.

Also, in order for Yao Ming to play overseas, many different Chinese authorities would have to agree to grant permission for him to go, including management of the Shanghai Sharks, officials of the CBA, and even representatives of the city government of Shanghai. These authorities weren't interested in the idea of Yao playing for a college team, however. As one official representing the Sharks commented in 1999, "He's under contract, and we'd like to train him more." At some point, he said, if the government allowed it, perhaps the Sharks would consider selling him to a foreign team. "The better he is, the better price we can sell him for," said the official. They weren't thinking of college for Yao; they were thinking of the NBA.

But Yao wasn't entirely sure that he wanted to go overseas. "I haven't really thought about it," he said when first asked by an American reporter if he wanted to play in the United States. "If my boss thinks it would be good for my development, I would go. Whatever you decide, you lose something."

That wasn't to say that Yao hadn't considered the possibility of joining the NBA. He was simply trying to see the decision from both sides. As he said, "If I stay in China, I lose the opportunity to go to the NBA. But if I go to the NBA, I lose the chance to serve my country. And my country is the most important thing."

Although he didn't have many material possessions in China, compared with most citizens, he was well taken care of, even wealthy. His housing and food were provided free of charge, and he received a salary of $61 per month, which was a great deal of money by Chinese standards. In addition, he received performance bonuses for playing in tournaments and on the national team that lifted his income to several thousand dollars a year. In China, that made him a rich young man. As one of his American teammates on the Sharks commented, "He'd be leaving everything. Here it's family and duty first. It's a huge cultural difference. Everything is a group decision. You do what's best for the group, not [for] the individual." And so far, it was probably best for Yao to remain in China. Almost everyone agreed that he wasn't yet good enough to make it in the NBA. He'd likely end up sitting on the bench.

The Chinese, however, were beginning to realize that the NBA might not be such a bad place for some Chinese players after all. In 1999, the Dallas Mavericks tried to draft Wang Zhizhi, who was only one year older and several inches shorter than Yao but a more polished player. The Mavericks knew that the Chinese were unlikely to allow Wang to play in the NBA, because he, like Yao, was on the national team and a star in the CBA. But they wanted the Chinese to start thinking about the possibility.

However, Chinese citizens can't simply decide to move to another country. Those who do move violate Chinese law. They are considered defectors, people who have committed a crime against the government. When Chinese officials didn't allow Wang Zhizhi to join the Mavericks, they became worried that he might defect. He didn't, but the officials realized that other players, including Yao Ming, might decide to take the risk if given the opportunity.

In the spring of 2000, Yao was scheduled to attend another Nike Camp in the States. But the Chinese government refused to let him go. It started training camp for the Chinese Olympic team early and said that Yao's schedule would not allow him to attend. The next time American audiences would see him play would be against their own national team in the Summer Olympic Games in Sydney, Australia.

Chinese officials and American-basketball representatives did not yet trust each other, but despite the Chinese's refusal to allow Yao to go to the camp, each side was beginning to reach out to the other. Nike employed thousands of people in its plants in

China. It had a great deal of influence with team and government officials. The Chinese were starting to realize that having some Chinese players in the NBA might not only help Chinese basketball, but also help the Chinese image all over the world. And the NBA looked at the enormous number of Chinese basketball fans and hoped to turn them into fans of the NBA and buyers of NBA products. But just as Yao had a great deal to learn about basketball, Chinese- and American-basketball officials still had a great deal to learn about each other.

Chapter Four:
2000–2001

Hopeful Olympian

Yao was disappointed that he was not allowed to go to the Nike Camp, but he was ready to focus his attention on training for the 2000 Olympics in Sydney, Australia. Chinese officials were optimistic that the team could make the medal round. They dreamed of playing Wang Zhizhi, Menk Bateer, and Yao Ming all at the same time in what they called "The Great Walking Wall."

Yao and his teammates worked hard at camp, but many of them realized that Chinese officials were far too optimistic. The Chinese style of play just couldn't compete with that of teams that emulated American basketball. At the same time, one player who might have helped the team, Ma Jian — easily the most talented guard in China — was still banned from the team by these same overoptimistic officials.

31

The Chinese national team and its officials got a wake-up call just before the Olympics. The NBA Ambassadors, a team composed of young American college graduates and NBA hopefuls, came to China to play the national team in three goodwill games. Although they were hardly the best players in America, the Ambassadors' athleticism and speed shocked the Chinese coaches.

Yao and Wang Zhizhi both played well, but the Ambassadors easily won all three contests. One observer commented that it was a shame that the team didn't have a real point guard to get the big men the basketball. As Ambassadors coach Tiny Archibald, a former NBA star, said, "Those two guys belong in the NBA right now." When they got the ball, Yao and Wang had been almost unstoppable. The problem was that they simply didn't get the ball often enough.

The Chinese team practiced long and hard for the Olympics — sometimes as long as four or five hours every day. Entering the Olympics, the Chinese still believed that their team could finish in the top eight teams in the world and had an outside chance at a medal. After all, only the American team had players as tall as Wang Zhizhi, Menk Bateer, and Yao Ming.

The officials who oversaw the basketball program believed that the more the team practiced, the better it would become. To a certain extent, that was true. But too much practice can make a team exhausted. That's what happened to the Chinese.

Professional players had been allowed to compete in the Olympics since 1992. For the 2000 Olympics, the United States had put together a so-called dream team primarily made up of NBA stars, such as Alonzo Mourning and Vince Carter. It was this squad that Yao and his teammates would face first. Although no one expected the Chinese team to win, basketball fans all over the world were curious to see how close the game would be.

At the start of the game, China jumped ahead to a 9–5 lead. Wang Zhizhi and Yao Ming controlled the inside. The Americans realized that the two big men could give them real trouble if they were able to play the whole game.

So the experienced American club went right after the two big men, hoping to trick them into making fouls. It worked. In the first five and a half minutes of the game, Wang Zhizhi picked up four fouls and the Chinese coach removed him from the game.

Now the Americans could focus on Yao Ming. But instead of going after him and getting him into foul trouble, they simply stayed out of his way. When the Americans had the ball, they tried to draw Yao away from the basket. When the Chinese had the ball, they put pressure on the guards so that they couldn't get the ball to Yao. When he did get the ball, he was usually either well covered or not in a very good position to take a shot.

The Americans slowly took control of the game. The Chinese guards simply weren't quick enough to compete with their American counterparts. The game remained close until late in the first half. Then the Chinese team ran out of gas. All those long practices had sapped the players' energy. Yao tried to do too much, but he, like Wang, was exhausted and made some foolish fouls. Early in the second half, he fouled out, and the Americans romped to a 119–72 win.

Despite their team's loss, Wang Zhizhi and Yao Ming had made people stand up and take notice. "I was impressed with both players," said American coach Rudy Tomjanovich, adding that Yao "has a really good future. I was impressed with how well he handled the ball. Usually, someone that big and that young can't do much with the ball, but he provided a good target, and he made some nice passes."

"We had to adjust to those guys," said American guard Ray Allen. "We sent Alonzo and Vin Baker at them to get them in foul trouble, and then our guards went to work."

Other observers wondered what would have happened had the Chinese not been so exhausted. One American athlete who had played in China described the Chinese team as "the most athletic foreign team you'll ever see. But you'll never know it because they're so tired."

The Chinese went on to win only two of their six Olympic contests, finishing in a disappointing tenth place. Four years before, in the 1996 Olympics, they had finished eighth with a much poorer team. But in the long run, their tenth place finish in 2000 may have been the best thing that ever happened, both for Chinese basketball and for Yao Ming.

Millions of Americans had watched Yao in the

Olympics, as had many NBA coaches and scouts. Everyone realized that he had the chance to be a huge star. Even though Wang Zhizhi was the more polished player, Yao's potential was unlimited. People began to imagine what it would be like for a player of Yao's size and skill to play in the NBA.

Although a handful of athletes as tall as Yao, or even taller, had played in the NBA, few of them were very skilled. Manute Bol of the Sudan stood seven feet seven. Although he was a good shot blocker, he was too skinny to guard most NBA big men, and he had a difficult time shooting. Others, like Utah's seven-foot, four-inch center, Mark Eaton, had the opposite problem. Eaton was so big that he was clumsy. Faster players simply went around him. Of all the really big men to play in the NBA, only seven-foot, four-inch Ralph Sampson had had talent as well as height. Many observers believed that Yao could be the same kind of player if he had a chance to improve his skills in the NBA.

After their disappointing performance in the Olympics, the Chinese were beginning to consider that possibility. They realized that their basketball program was going backward and that, unless their players faced better competition and utilized more-modern training methods, they were unlikely to be threatening in international competition. China was scheduled to host the 2008 Summer Olympics, and it hoped to showcase its athletes, particularly its basketball team, in front of the world. The team had plenty of incentive to improve.

In the 2000–2001 season of the Chinese Basketball Association, Yao Ming came of age. Yao and Wang Zhizhi thrilled Chinese fans with their spectacular play as each player's performance seemed to inspire the other. Wang averaged nearly 25 points per game. But Yao was even better. He averaged almost 28 points and won the league MVP Award — an honor that had gone to Wang in each of the previous three seasons.

Both players led their teams to the championship finals. Many expected Yao's Shanghai Sharks to wrest the championship from the defending champs, Wang's Bayi Rockets. But in a thrilling series that went to the final game, Wang, scoring forty points in the finale, led his team to victory.

The series captivated Chinese basketball fans. The game had never been more popular.

All the while, Chinese and American representatives had been discussing Wang's future. After being drafted by Dallas, Wang had enlisted an American representative, Bill Duffy, to negotiate with Chinese authorities and try to convince them to allow him to play in the NBA.

At length, they worked out a deal for him to play for Dallas. The NBA would pay a fee to Wang's team and, in exchange, agreed to allow him to return to play for China in international competitions. The two nations also agreed to allow some Chinese coaches to come to the United States to learn new coaching techniques and to permit American players and coaches to visit China and help teach the Chinese how to play. Although the agreement was just for one year and only affected Wang, it was an important step. All of a sudden, Yao Ming's future seemed much brighter.

If Wang Zhizhi was going to be the first Chinese player in the NBA, Yao Ming was determined to be the next.

Chapter Five:
2001-2002

The Chinese Rocket

Yao hoped that his chance to follow Wang Zhizhi to the NBA would happen quickly. But the Chinese weren't in a rush, and Yao's situation was somewhat different. Wang had played for a team sponsored by a branch of the Chinese government, the People's Liberation Army. It was relatively easy for him to get permission to leave. The government just had to say "yes."

But Yao Ming's team, the Shanghai Sharks, was sponsored by the Shanghai government and by private investors. All of those groups, as well as the Chinese Basketball Association and the government-sponsored national team, had to agree to any arrangement that would allow Yao to enter the NBA.

Increasingly, the Sharks and the Chinese officials were becoming aware of what it would mean for Yao to leave China and play in the NBA. Although the Sharks seemed willing to part with their young star at some point, for the time being, they were more interested in winning the CBA championship.

Yao flourished in the 2001–2002 season. No player in the league could stop him. In 34 regular-season games, he averaged more than 32 points per game and 19 rebounds. He could have scored even more, but Yao often passed the ball off or left the game early when the Sharks were way ahead. The Sharks, too, were nearly unbeatable, romping their way to first place in the CBA.

They reached the finals in the playoffs, facing the Bayi Rockets. The Rockets had been the top team for six years in a row and had beaten the Sharks in the championship in 2000. Things would be different this time, in large part due to Yao's performance.

He saved his best game for last. In the Sharks' championship-clinching win over Bayi, Yao was almost perfect. Twenty-one times he went to the basket, impressing fans with a variety of moves that included long jump shots, reverse lay-ups, and dunks. And twenty-one times Yao Ming put the ball in the basket, finishing with 44 points on perfect 21-of-21 shooting as the Sharks won 123–122.

After the game, it was clear that Yao had nothing left to prove in Chinese basketball. The Sharks and Chinese officials were beginning to reach the same conclusion. In April 2002, the Sharks finally gave Yao permission to enter the NBA. The Shanghai government and national team officials indicated that they, too, would be willing to allow Yao to go.

Yao traveled to the United States and went to Chicago, where the NBA arranged for him to participate in a special workout for NBA coaches and scouts. The NBA draft lottery and draft were rapidly approaching, and every team had some interest in Yao. But no one as yet was really certain where Yao would fit in the draft. During the workout, it became clear that Yao would be one of the top picks. In the nearly empty gym, working out alone and against other players, Yao put on a clinic that highlighted all of his skills.

He first demonstrated his running ability and ball-handing skills, dribbling up and down the court. Then he would stop and dribble the ball between his legs, feinting first one way and then another, as if he were playing against an invisible opponent.

Up in the stands, the NBA coaches and scouts watched in awe. They had never seen a player as tall as Yao do the things that he was doing.

Then he started shooting the ball, lofting up jump shot after jump shot from fifteen, twenty, even twenty-five feet from the basket. Shot after shot rained down through the hoop.

And when Yao moved under the basket, he was no less impressive. He proved that he could start with his back to the basket, fake, and go to the hoop for jams or lay-ups with either hand. On the rare occasions that he missed, he jumped high above the rim to pull down the ball. All the coaches and scouts in the stands began imagining Yao playing for their team.

When he began scrimmaging against an opponent, he was only slightly less impressive. Chris Christofferson, a seven-foot, two-inch center who had played for the University of Oregon, was recruited to play opposite Yao.

Christofferson, who was much heavier, several years older, and more experienced, showed that Yao still had some learning to do. Yao had some trouble when Christofferson played the rough style of the NBA. But at the same time, he impressed observers with his tenacity. He didn't back down or get frustrated, and he demonstrated a great deal of stamina.

Everyone was impressed. After the workout, NBA Hall of Fame legend Jerry West, representing the Memphis Grizzlies, was asked if Yao would be physical enough to succeed in the NBA. West didn't think it would be a problem, saying, "How many good low-post centers are there in the NBA? Not that many. The biggest adjustment will be the level of competition." West believed that Yao had the skills to play in the NBA.

Most observers echoed the comments of Houston Rockets general manager Carroll Dawson. He described Yao as "very impressive. Tremendous size. Shot the ball and ran well. He dribbled with both hands very well. I think you have to think about him if you got the first pick."

When Rockets fans heard that, they paid attention. Since winning the NBA championship in 1994, the franchise had fallen on hard times and was looking toward the upcoming draft for some help. They

43

hadn't made the playoffs in three years. As one of the worst teams in the league in the 2001–2002 NBA season, the Rockets were eligible for the NBA draft lottery that determined which team would receive the first pick. Although the Rockets had about one chance in ten of winning the lottery for the first pick, their fans were still hopeful.

The Rockets had been lucky before. In 1983 and 1984, they had received the first picks, choosing seven-foot, four-inch Ralph Sampson in 1983 and six-foot, eleven-inch center Hakeem Olajuwon in 1984. The "Twin Towers," as the two players were called, made the team an instant contender in the NBA, and in 1994, Olajuwon led the team to its first championship. If the Rockets could somehow get Yao Ming, perhaps he could eventually lead them to another championship.

The lottery draw was held during the playoffs in late May. When NBA commissioner David Stern announced that the Rockets had beaten the odds and won the first pick, Rockets fans everywhere broke out in cheers.

But the Rockets hadn't yet decided whom to select. The team was interested in about a half dozen players in addition to Yao.

Yao was intriguing, but he also represented a risk. Although the Chinese had given every sign that they would allow Yao to play in the NBA, nothing was official, and the Rockets knew that the Chinese could change their minds in an instant. And no one could predict how Yao would react when he became an instant millionaire or if he would continue to improve. A number of critics thought that the Rockets would be wasting their pick on Yao. While the Rockets had a month to make their decision, Yao was anxious to learn where he would be playing.

His cousin, Erick Zhang, was a graduate student in Chicago, and Yao asked him to help him in negotiations with both the Chinese and the Americans. Zhang then asked a college professor, John Huizenga, for assistance. No matter where Yao played, they wanted to make sure that he got a fair contract.

Meanwhile, the Rockets asked Yao to come to Houston to work out for the team. While there, he met with coach Rudy Tomjanovich and other Rockets officials. After the meeting, the team reached an understanding. In early June, they decided to select Yao Ming with the first pick in the draft if they could be sure that the Chinese would allow him to play.

Now the Rockets, Erick Zhang, and NBA officials began working together to hammer out the details that would allow Yao to come to the United States. They sent letters to Chinese officials and then made plans to travel to China and meet face-to-face.

One Rockets official summed up the situation: "The Chinese want to make sure Yao Ming is available for the Chinese national team when it competes internationally, and we need him here [in the United States] frequently enough to be the best player he can be." It wouldn't do the Rockets much good to sign Yao if he wasn't able to play very much, just as it wouldn't help the Chinese if he didn't get enough experience in the United States to improve his game.

Several Rockets officials, including Coach Tomjanovich, traveled to China to meet with the management of both the Sharks and the CBA. While the negotiation was taking place, Tomjanovich had the opportunity to meet Yao again and speak with him for a long time. He came away very impressed.

"He had a great personality," Tomjanovich said. "He really opened up after a while. He asked about the players on our team. Then we went on the floor a little bit and we talked about a couple of basketball things. I'm excited. I didn't know what to expect when we got here, but I'm real encouraged." Of course, the two had to talk through a translator because Yao still knew very little English and Tomjanovich no Chinese.

During that same visit, Yao's parents informed Tomjanovich that former Rockets star Hakeem Olajuwon was their son's favorite player, and Tomjanovich told them all about Houston. In the Houston metropolitan area, there are more than 200,000 people of Asian descent, including thousands of Chinese. The Americans assured Yao's parents that their son would be comfortable in Houston.

At the end of the visit, the Rockets and the Chinese reached a formal agreement allowing Yao to play in the United States. The Chinese agreed that he could play for the Rockets during the regular season and playoffs. In exchange, the Rockets agreed to make Yao available for important international tournaments. And Yao signed a letter promising to play for his country and send half of his salary back to China. At the end of all the talking, Yao Ming would be a Houston Rocket.

A few days before the draft, the Rockets gave videotapes of Yao Ming playing basketball to current members of the team. While many of them knew that the Rockets were going to draft Yao, few had seen him play.

"This guy can move," said Rockets guard Moochie Norris, speaking for the team. "He's skilled, he's crafty with the ball. He's good around the basket. He can block shots. Athletic. Run the floor. I like him. I'm excited." All of a sudden, the Rockets felt as if they were a new team.

The NBA draft took place on June 26, 2002. To no one's surprise, the Rockets announced that they had chosen Yao Ming. He became the first foreign player who hadn't played basketball at an American college to be selected as the number one draft pick.

Yao watched the draft on television with his family in Beijing, China, where he was training with the national team for a tournament. When he met with reporters afterward, he summed up his feelings by saying, "It's a big day. It's a new beginning for me."

Then someone asked him if he was looking forward to playing against Shaquille O'Neal, the powerful center for the Los Angeles Lakers and arguably the best center in the world. Yao Ming startled the observer with his answer.

"He is a mountain in my way," he said. "I will try to conquer it by any means. My first tries may turn out to be failures, but I will continue with others."

Clearly, Yao Ming wasn't going to be satisfied just playing in the NBA. He wanted to be a star.

Chapter Six:
2002

Starting Slow

While the Rockets and Yao's representative began negotiating his contract, Yao had to fulfill his commitments to the Chinese national team, including playing in the international world championships. As part of the team's preparations, it played a series of exhibitions against other national teams. On August 16, it played in Vancouver against the Canadian team. The game would be Yao's first appearance in North America and drew a great deal of attention. The Canadian team, led by Dallas Mavericks star guard Steve Nash, was deep and talented. The game would provide a good test for Yao.

The crowd began arriving early at the arena. Observers were surprised to see so many Chinese fans in the crowd. Although Vancouver has a sizable Chi-

nese population, few Chinese had attended basketball games in the city before. But at this game, more
Chinese flags waved in the crowd than Canadian
ones. And in the pre-game introductions, Yao received the loudest cheers from the crowd.

In the game's opening minutes, it became clear
that the Canadian team was faster and more skilled
than the Chinese team. Although Yao towered over
Canadian center Richard Anderson, his teammates
had a hard time getting him the ball. But when they
did, he didn't disappoint.

Seven minutes into the game, Yao finally got the
ball down low. Anderson leaned on him heavily, but
Yao held his ground. Then, quick as a wink, he made
his move. With the ball held between his hands, Yao
faked one way. Anderson shifted slightly, giving Yao
just the advantage that he needed. He spun in the
opposite direction and jumped to the basket, raising
the ball high above his head.

Anderson tried to react and went up with Yao,
desperately trying to stop him. But the Canadian
was powerless. Even though he bumped into Yao
and struck him across the arms, Yao would not be

denied. Yao slammed the ball through the hoop for a basket. As he did, the referee blew his whistle and called a foul on Anderson.

The crowd jumped to its feet. As his fans roared their approval, Yao calmly sank the free throw to complete the three-point play.

Unfortunately for Yao, his teammates continued to have a hard time getting him the ball. But when they did, he was deadly, making six shots plus five free throws to finish with 17 points. Although the Canadians rarely challenged him inside, he also blocked five shots and made three steals. Still, China was overmatched and lost the game, 94–66.

Coach Tomjanovich had been watching closely from the stands. "I like what I saw," he said. But Yao knew he could have played better. He thought that he knew one way he could improve.

"I need more weight training," he said. Even against the smaller Canadian players, Yao had difficulty maintaining position. To succeed in the NBA, he knew that he would have to get much stronger.

In the meantime, he continued to be impressive on the Chinese national team. In the world championships played in Indianapolis, he made the all-tournament team after averaging 21 points a game, including a high of 38 versus Algeria. Then he traveled to Korea for the Asian Games.

When that tournament ended in late October, Yao was finally free to join the Rockets. He signed his contract with the Rockets for an incredible $17.8 million dollars over four seasons. Then he made his way to the United States to join his new teammates at the Rockets training camp. They had already been practicing for weeks. The regular season was only ten days away. Yao would have to learn fast.

Everyone tried to make the transition as easy as possible. Although Yao had been busy playing with the national team, his cousin, Erick Zhang, made arrangements for Yao and his parents to live together in West Houston. He also hired a translator, Colin Pine, to help Yao at practice and with the media. As much as they could, the Rockets made Yao feel comfortable. But with the season starting so soon, they had to concentrate on the game. There wasn't much time to get to know their newest teammate.

Not that Yao needed much time. From his first practice on October 21, Yao fit right in. With translator Colin Pine standing alongside him during breaks in the action, Yao patiently began learning the Rockets' plays. The Rockets hadn't had a dominant center since Hakeem Olajuwon had played for the team. They even dusted off a few old plays designed for Olajuwon to take advantage of their new player's talents.

The Rockets planned to take things slowly with Yao. Everything was new to him, and they didn't want him to feel overwhelmed. But Yao surprised his teammates by adapting easily. After being shown something once, he understood what the Rockets wanted him to do. It seemed as if basketball was the universal language.

Just three days later, on October 23, he made his debut in a Rockets exhibition game in San Antonio against the San Antonio Spurs. The Spurs' starting lineup featured two seven-footers — veteran and former MVP David Robinson and 2001–2002 MVP Tim Duncan — who was considered by some to be even better than Shaquille O'Neal.

At the start of the game, Yao was nervous. The Rockets kept him on the bench for a few minutes before tapping him on the shoulder and putting him in. Within a few minutes, he showed both his vast potential and how much he had to learn.

On several occasions, David Robinson got the ball and started to drive toward the basket. In stepped Yao, moving in front of the former MVP. Each time, Robinson thought better of shooting in close and instead stepped back for a jump shot.

Yao was clearly an intimidating presence. But he also struggled to keep up, and he wasn't nearly as strong as his counterparts. In thirteen minutes of play, he fell to the ground three times.

Yao finished with six points and four rebounds. But he also picked up three fouls in his first five minutes. On one foul, the far more experienced Robinson tricked him, hooking Yao with one arm, then falling to the ground as Yao tried to pull free, making it appear as if Yao had pushed him.

Even though the Rockets lost the exhibition 80–79, Yao was still pleased to have his first game behind him. "My dream starts here," he said.

David Robinson agreed. The old veteran had seen enough. "He's going to be good," he said. "He's going to have an impact in this league."

The next night, Yao had an impact in Houston. He played on his home court for the first time in another exhibition game, this time against the Philadelphia 76ers.

Coach Tomjanovich was still cautious with his young star and kept him out of the game in the first quarter. When Tomjanovich finally put him in, the crowd gave Yao a thirty-second ovation. Every time he touched the ball, they roared. Every time he was fouled or Tomjanovich pulled him from the game, they booed. And every time he scored or pulled down a rebound, they went nuts.

He played much better than the night before. Early in his appearance, he got the ball near the basket. Philadelphia's Art Long blocked his way to the basket.

As Yao backed in, he appeared to be in too deep to take a shot. Long shifted position to stop Yao from moving back out. That's when the rookie made his move. In a flash, Yao used a spin move that sent him underneath the basket. Then he reached out his long arm and deftly tossed in a reverse lay-up.

The 76ers star forward Glenn Robinson was im-

Yao Ming, member of the Chinese Basketball Association's Shanghai Sharks, holds up the championship trophy that his team won in April 2002.

Slam dunk! China's Yao Ming skies over a player from Kuwait
during the Asian Men's Basketball Games in 2002.

In 2002, Houston Rockets coach Rudy Tomjanovich talks with Yao Ming just before Yao's first NBA start.

AP/Wide World Photos

Yao proves that big men can dribble!

Fans hold up signs for their newest favorite player, Yao Ming.

Yao Ming searches for the open man in a game against the
Denver Nuggets in 2003.

Yao soars to the net over a Phoenix Sun.

2003 All-Stars Michael Jordan, Yao Ming, and others mix it up on the court.

The battle of the big men: Shaquille O'Neal versus Yao Ming!

Yao Ming poses with soccer players Jorg Albertz and Qi Hong prior to the "Stars vs. SARS" three-hour benefit telethon in Shanghai.

Yao Ming's Career Stats

Year	Team	Games	Rebounds	Assists	Blocks	Field-Goal Percentage	Points	Points per Game
1997-98	Shanghai Sharks	21	175	13	N/A	.615	210	10.0
1998-99	Shanghai Sharks	12	155	7	N/A	.585	251	20.9
1999-2000	Shanghai Sharks	33	480	57	N/A	.585	699	21.2
2000-2001	Shanghai Sharks	22	426	48	N/A	.678	596	27.1
2001-2002	Shanghai Sharks	34	645	98	N/A	.721	1102	32.4
2002-2003	Houston Rockets	82	675	137	147	.498	1104	13.5

Yao Ming's Career Highlights

1999–2000:
Member of the Chinese national basketball team

2000–2001:
Member of the Chinese national basketball team
Member of the Chinese Basketball Association All-Star team

2001–2002:
Member of the Chinese national basketball team
Member of the Chinese Basketball Association All-Star team
Voted Most Valuable Player of the Chinese Basketball Association
Voted Most Valuable Player of the Asian Championships
Member of the Chinese Basketball Association
    Championship team

2002–2003:

Chosen by the Houston Rockets with the first overall pick in
the 2002 NBA Draft

NBA Rookie of the Month for December and February

Western Division's starting center for the NBA All-Star Game

Member of the NBA All-Rookie First Team

pressed with the maneuver. "To get a guy that big to do a baseline move like that — it's unbelievable," he said.

Yao had more unbelievable moves still to come. Later in the game, he crashed the boards following a shot by Rockets star guard Steve Francis. As the ball bounced out of the hoop, Yao deftly tapped it back in for another two points.

Philadelphia rapidly inbounded the ball after the basket. Guard Allen Iverson, perhaps the fastest player and best ball-handler in the league, streaked down the court, hoping to surprise the Rockets. Instead, he received a surprise. As he reached the opposite end of the court, he found Yao waiting for him.

Yao had run hard down the court right after he'd scored. When Iverson tried to scoot past him, Yao reached out and swatted the ball away for a clean steal.

The crowd went crazy. Yao-mania was already in full swing.

In 24 minutes, Yao scored 13 points, pulled down five rebounds, and blocked two shots. Coach Tomjanovich paid him a compliment after the game when he said simply, "He can play." In only a week, Yao had made great strides. But he was still learning the system and adjusting to life in America.

But the regular season wouldn't wait. After waiting to play in the NBA for much of his life, Yao Ming would finally get his chance.

Chapter Seven:
2002

Growing Pains

Although Yao Ming received a great deal of attention, he wasn't the only talented player on the Rockets. Sharp-shooting guard Steve Francis was an emerging star. Young Eddie Griffin and Kelvin Cato were both potential front-court threats, and the Rockets were optimistic about the career of the club's second first-round pick, rookie Bostjian Nachbar, a native of Slovakia.

All the Rockets lacked was experience. But that would come quickly in the NBA.

The team opened the regular season in Indianapolis on October 30 against the Pacers. Although neither team was considered to be championship caliber, the presence of Yao Ming attracted the attention of basketball fans all over the country.

Unfortunately, the Rockets had to begin the season short-handed. Three players missed the game because of injuries, and another, Maurice Taylor, was serving a brief suspension. All four played either forward or center, leaving the Rockets badly undermanned. They began the game with only nine available players.

It was hardly the perfect situation for Yao's debut. The team got off to a slow start. When Yao entered the game, the Rockets were already far behind. He didn't do much to help them. In eleven minutes, he barely touched the ball, taking only one shot, which he missed, and pulling down only two rebounds. Despite a career-high 39 points from Steve Francis, the Rockets lost, 91–82.

Yao was disappointed with his playing. "There are some things I regret about tonight," he admitted afterward. "But this is just the beginning."

His teammates defended him to the press, telling reporters that, despite his slow start, Yao could play. And a handful of reporters from China told their American counterparts that Yao's first game in the CBA had been very similar.

But some observers weren't very kind, calling him

things like "The Great Bust of China" and concluding that he couldn't play at all. One reporter wrote that "Inside of three or four years he'll be history. . . . Manute Bol has a better chance of playing hockey than Yao does of having an All-Star career." And when Yao failed to score or improve much in the Rockets' second game, the criticism increased. Outspoken NBA analyst and former All-Star Charles Barkley predicted that Yao would never score as many as nineteen points in a game.

Yao had confidence in his ability, but it still hurt to be criticized. Coach Tomjanovich just kept reminding everyone that Yao had missed most of training camp and was still adjusting to the speed of the game.

Houston fans weren't ready to give up on their team either. When the Rockets played their first game in Houston against the Toronto Raptors, the arena was packed. There hadn't been so much excitement about a basketball game in Houston in years. When the youthful Rockets came out to the court for warm-ups, they heard the reception from the crowd and immediately started feeling pumped up and excited.

The team jumped out to a quick lead. But less than four minutes into the game, starting center Kelvin Cato picked up his second foul. Coach Tomjanovich called on Yao.

Yao received a raucous standing ovation when he trotted onto the court. He tried to stay calm and focus on his play. A few moments after entering the game, he got the ball and put up a short jumper. The ball rolled around the rim and then fell out. The crowd groaned.

But a moment later, Yao changed those groans to shouts of delight. He got the ball again in the middle of the free-throw lane, only six or eight feet from the basket. Without hesitating, he made his move, spinning to the baseline in a flash. He then turned back to the basket, went straight up, and lofted a soft jump shot over the hands of the startled defender. The ball soared to the hoop in a soft arc as Yao floated back to the ground.

Swish!

The crowd erupted with joy. It was the kind of play that demonstrated that Yao was just beginning to harness his potential. Only a handful of centers in the league could make the same move. On the

Houston bench, Coach Tomjanovich pumped his fist in approval.

Later in the half, Yao made another spectacular play. Gathering the ball in down low, Yao went up, then brought the ball back down and tossed up an underhanded lay-up around a defender. The crowd roared again.

Meanwhile, the Rockets raced ahead by a wide margin. The Raptors became tentative on offense, as if no one wanted to challenge Yao beneath the basket.

Early in the second half, Yao added to his growing resume of highlight-quality plays. He dropped in a fadeaway hook shot in the third quarter, tossing the ball over his head while falling away from the basket.

But two other plays really got the crowd going. The Raptors' Morris Peterson stormed down the lane, determined to score. He pulled up short of the basket and went up. Yao stretched out his arm and leaped to challenge the shot. Peterson reached the apex of his jump, but Yao was still rising. His arm loomed over the smaller player. Peterson shot anyway, trying to arc the ball over Yao. The big man swatted it away for his first blocked shot.

Yet there was still one thing he hadn't done in a game yet: dunk the ball.

He had his chance at the start of the fourth quarter when the ball rolled free under the basket. Yao scooped it up and seemingly without thinking went straight to the hoop. Well, not exactly straight to the hoop, but up and over it. Yao is so tall that when he jumps in the air he can almost look down into the basket. He barely needs to jump in order to touch the rim. This time, he jumped as high as he could and jammed the ball in.

As the crowd roared, a great feeling of joy came over Yao. He didn't smile on the court, but he was growing more confident by the moment.

The Rockets cruised to a 88–76 win. After the game, Yao, who had scored eight points and pulled down four rebounds, was all everyone wanted to talk about. Teammate Steve Francis said, "He stepped up. I thought Yao brought a lot to the table tonight with his intensity."

Yao hoped that every game would go as smoothly, but that was not possible. In the Rockets' next game, against Seattle, they fell behind early. Yao barely played, and when he did, he failed to score and picked up several quick fouls.

He admitted that at times he was just trying too hard. "There is a lot of pressure on me," he said. "It's something I have to deal with. I don't think I've been able to show the best of my abilities yet. I'm not quite used to the speed of the game, especially on offense."

But Yao also revealed a rare understanding of the game. "Basketball is not something you can talk about: it's an action through which you can show people. I just think I need to show them on the court."

That was something he was just about ready to do.

Chapter Eight:
2002

Living in America

For all the adjustments that Yao had to make on the basketball court, the biggest challenges he faced were off the court. Although he had traveled widely as a member of the Chinese national team, American life was still a mystery to him.

In China, for instance, Yao didn't have a car; few Chinese citizens did. When he had to go somewhere in Shanghai, he either took the bus or rode his bicycle. One of the first things that he wanted to do when he arrived in the United States was learn to drive.

That was easier said than done. Yao could hardly fit in most cars, and he didn't know the first thing about traffic laws or how to read road signs. Nevertheless, soon after arriving in the United States, he began learning to drive an SUV.

Another big adjustment he had to make was dealing with the intense interest that everyone had in him, both because of his height and because of his Chinese background. Almost immediately, Yao became a fan favorite. Everyone wanted his autograph or to have their picture taken with him. (Standing next to Yao, most people who were considered tall looked short.) Such attention was distracting and made Yao uncomfortable at times.

He also had to adjust to the media. In China, only a few reporters covered him, and their access was extremely limited. But in the United States, there were sometimes as many as fifty reporters at a Rockets practice, and even more at games. And the reporters weren't just American, either. People all over the world wanted to know about Yao. As one reporter noted, "He's probably one of the most swamped people in the world. The press follows him everywhere."

Yao quickly learned that different reporters would ask the same kinds of questions over and over. One question that Yao was constantly asked was if he liked American food. Most people had the impression that in China, all he had ever eaten was food identical to that ordered at a Chinese restaurant. They didn't realize that Yao had traveled the world and that the food people eat in China isn't precisely the same as the food served in Chinese restaurants, just as American food isn't precisely the same as what is available in American fast-food restaurants.

Still, Yao answered all such questions politely. For the record, he really enjoys steak, cheese and mushroom pizza, and chocolate ice cream.

One way that Yao dealt with the media was by making jokes. When he was asked a really silly question, he would give a silly answer. On one occasion, for instance, he was asked what the biggest difference between playing basketball in the NBA and in China was.

"We speak English here," he quipped. "They speak Chinese in China."

On another occasion, he was asked what the easiest part about living in the United States was.

"Sleeping," deadpanned Yao. And he was half serious. He was playing a lot of basketball, and there were always demands on his time. Whenever anyone asked him how he was doing, he always answered, "Tired."

Many people in and around the NBA couldn't believe how well Yao adjusted to all the media pressure and how polite and caring he was. He even sent cards, thank-you notes, and small gifts to Rockets officials, his teammates, and even his opponents! As one member of the Rockets front office said after receiving a card, "That's the first time an NBA player has ever sent me anything." Unlike many other NBA players, Yao appreciated everything about his new life.

In many ways, he's just like any other twenty-two-year-old. He likes video games, especially those that feature a lot of action and adventure. He enjoys the *Star Wars* movies. He likes to play basketball, be with his family, and relax.

Off the court, even someone seven feet five is just another person. But on the court, the NBA was quickly learning that Yao Ming was someone special. Just as Yao had to adapt to life in America, players in the NBA would soon find out that they were going to have to adapt to life with Yao.

Chapter Nine:
2002

Coming Up Big

Ever since the beginning of the season, many basketball fans had looked forward to seeing Yao Ming play against the Los Angeles Lakers and their star center, Shaquille O'Neal. In the off-season, Shaq had even talked about how much he was looking forward to the match-up, promising that he would dominate the taller player.

But just before the season started, O'Neal underwent minor surgery on his big toe. When the Rockets came to Los Angeles on November 17 to take on the Lakers for the first time that season, O'Neal wasn't able to play.

The game still drew a great deal of attention. The Lakers, after all, were defending NBA champions. The young Rockets were excited to play them, even if Shaquille O'Neal was on the bench. When the game began, their enthusiasm showed. They matched the Lakers shot for shot.

And when Yao entered the game, he was like a different player. Almost overnight it seemed as if he finally understood the pace of play in the NBA. On defense, he was rarely out of position. He stayed away from stupid fouls. And on offense, he forced the Lakers to pay attention to him.

Entering the fourth quarter, the Rockets trailed by only five points. If they played hard, they still had a chance to beat the defending champs. They did just that, hitting their first seven shots to go ahead. Of these fourteen points, the two scored by Yao were the most dramatic.

The play started as a fast break. Steve Francis took off down the court with the ball and noticed that Yao was sprinting ahead of him. At the perfect moment, Yao started to cut toward the hoop, anticipating the play that Francis hoped to make. Francis saw a small opening to Yao in the passing lane. He fired a bounce pass that threaded its way between defenders and hit Yao in full stride.

Yao gathered the ball in his hands and left the ground, soaring to the hoop. He was too far out to dunk the ball, so he smoothly scooped it toward the basket and let it roll off his fingers and into the net. It was a spectacular shot that even had Lakers fans smiling.

From there, the game went back and forth. With a minute left, the Rockets nursed a one-point lead. The Rockets' Juaquin Hawkins had the ball and drove toward the hoop. As he did, the Lakers defense collapsed toward him, cutting off his path to the basket.

Yao sensed what was happening. As the defenders moved toward Hawkins, Yao cut to the hoop. Hawkins saw him and fired a quick pass. Yao didn't hesitate.

He went straight up, stretched out toward the basket, and slammed the ball through as a defender crashed into him for a foul. The Rockets now led by three — and by four as Yao calmly sank his free throw to complete the three-point play. The Rockets held on to win 93–89.

After the game, everyone seemed to realize that Yao Ming, who had scored twenty points while shooting a perfect 9-for-9 from the field, had made the difference.

"There was never any doubt in our minds that he could play," said teammate Maurice Taylor. "The reason we won was the buckets he had down the stretch."

"You couldn't ask for anything more from him," added Steve Francis. "He gave us a heck of a boost. I was just glad he was aggressive and dunking the ball. In his culture, you don't dunk the ball. But we've been on him from day one."

Coach Tomjanovich couldn't help but smile after the game as the press gathered around him and peppered him with questions about Yao Ming. Although he resisted the temptation to tell everyone "I told you so," he did quip, "He's been doing all those things in practice." Now that he was doing them in games, the sky was the limit.

Any lingering questions over whether or not Yao could play were answered definitively a few nights later in Dallas. The Rockets' arch rivals, the Dallas Mavericks, held a record of 11–0. Many people thought that the Mavericks were the best team in the NBA. Moreover, at seven feet six, their center, Shawn Bradley, was actually taller than Yao. Not a powerhouse on offense, he was a good defensive player. Many expected him to shut down the Rockets center.

Someone forgot to tell that to Yao Ming. Although his teammates struggled all night, Yao was virtually unstoppable. He scored thirty points, including twenty-one in the first half of the game. He made his points on hook shots, dunk shots, soft jumpers and tip-ins. After scoring seven points in the first quarter of the game, the Mavericks had to double-team him and give Bradley some help. In addition, Yao pulled down sixteen rebounds. Although the Rockets lost 103–90, Yao was the talk of the game.

Incredibly, with that game he came within one basket of setting an NBA record. After making 10 out of 12 shots, Yao's shooting record in his past five games was a remarkable 30 of 34, a .882 shooting percentage. In over fifty years of play, only one other player, the great Wilt Chamberlain, had ever shot more accurately over a five-game period.

But Yao was characteristically humble after the game. "You have to understand," he said, "I play this game in two parts. One part is the enjoyment of playing. The other part is, of course, winning. Today I achieved half of that."

Something incredible was happening. As Yao proved that he could play, he suddenly became the most popular player in the league, not only in the United States, but also all over the world.

His fine play made him much more relaxed. At press conferences, despite the awkwardness of answering every question through his translator, Yao began cracking more jokes. After the Dallas game, for instance, he quipped that after playing against Bradley, "Now I know I'm not the skinniest player in the NBA."

Wherever Yao went, crowds of people followed. Rockets officials noticed that more and more Chinese fans and people from other Asian countries began showing up at his games. Only a few Asian athletes had ever before succeeded in the United States, but none had been as big a star as Yao Ming.

And China was officially crazy over Yao. His games were broadcast back to China, where they drew enormous numbers of viewers. The NBA began selling Yao Ming jerseys in China. Soon it was almost impossible to walk down a street in a major Chinese city without seeing someone wearing one.

When the Rockets beat the Washington Wizards in their next game to make their record 7–4, even Wizards legend Michael Jordan was impressed. After all, Yao outscored Jordan 18 to 8 and set a career high with eight blocked shots.

"He's for real," Jordan said.

Doug Collins, the Wizards' coach, agreed. "Historically, what happens with big men in the league is they have a game or two like that and the light goes on," he said. "Then, watch out."

The big test for Yao came a little over a week later when the Rockets played against the San Antonio Spurs. Armed with big men Tim Duncan and David Robinson as well as other talented players, the Spurs were one of the best teams in the league. They had defeated the Rockets in 15 of their previous 16 games.

Yao hadn't forgotten how Duncan and Robinson had dominated him in his first exhibition game. He was determined to play better.

Early in the game, his teammates learned just how determined. Yao was dominant. He didn't just outplay Duncan and Robinson individually; he outplayed them together. In one memorable moment late in the game, he left teammates, opponents, and fans in awe.

Steve Francis took a shot, and the ball hit the rim and bounced back out. Yao went up for the rebound, leaving Duncan and Robinson behind. But he didn't catch the ball and shoot a short jumper or lay the ball into the basket. Instead, he *punched* it. Like a volleyball player spiking the ball, Yao went high into the air and slammed the ball with his fist into the basket as hard as he could. The ball thundered through the hoop and then bounced high into the air as the crowd first gasped, then roared.

The Spurs called an immediate time-out. As Yao trotted over to the bench, his teammates failed to greet him with high fives or hand slaps. They, too, were stunned by his power. None of them had ever seen a player do what he'd done before.

"I hope they don't think I'm a monster," quipped Yao after the game. They didn't, but the Spurs may well have felt that way about him. After all, he had destroyed the two former MVPs during the Rockets 89–75 win, scoring 27 points and pulling down 18 rebounds — more than Duncan and Robinson combined.

All of a sudden, there seemed no limit to just how good Yao Ming could become. As surprising as that was to some, what really shocked many was how fast it was happening. While the Rockets had expected Yao to become a star, they had never expected it to happen in his first month in the league!

Some of the greatest former players in the league were now calling Yao a special player. Television commentator Bill Walton, one of the best NBA centers ever before his career was cut short by injuries, said simply, "There is no limit to what he can accomplish." Walton was even more impressed by Yao's intelligence than he was by his skill. Walton compared him to Larry Bird, saying that Yao was "so far ahead of everyone else mentally. Yao Ming has the potential, the capability, of changing the future of basketball."

That was a great deal of responsibility. So far, however, Yao Ming had shown that he was up to the task. But the season was far from over—and greater challenges awaited the NBA rookie.

Chapter Ten:
2002–2003

Yao versus Shaq

As big as Yao was on the court, he was becoming even bigger off the court. Rockets games were suddenly sell-outs wherever they played. The youthful team loved the attention. For the past few years, hardly anyone wanted to see them play, and they had grown accustomed to playing in front of unenthusiastic crowds.

Now, even when the Rockets played on the road, the crowds were huge. Moreover, the majority of fans usually cheered for Yao and the Rockets. In the fan balloting for the All-Star game, Yao had more votes than any other player in the league.

Yao's picture suddenly started appearing on magazine covers. Journalists from all over the country began following the Rockets so that they could write stories about Yao. Two Houston songwriters, Chance McClain and Kevin Ryan, even wrote a rap song about Yao called "It's a Ming Thing." The Rockets Power Dancers, a group of women who dance for the crowd during time-outs, developed a routine based on the song. Every time it was played at the Rockets' home arena, the crowd went crazy.

The tune even made it to China. Every Rockets game was broadcast live, which meant that people there watched the games at dawn. As one of the songwriters said, "They call it 'Breakfast with Yao' and play our song before each game."

Yet despite all the attention, Yao somehow managed to keep everything in perspective. It helped to have his mother staying with him at his home in the Houston suburbs. After every game, she made sure that he had something to eat and did everything she could to help him relax. As a world-class athlete herself, she knew how difficult his life could be.

Translator Colin Pine also stayed with Yao: While he still translated for the Rocket, he had also been hired to help Yao learn English so that his services eventually wouldn't be needed. Yao would even joke that he couldn't wait to fire him.

It also helped that Yao was becoming friends with his teammates. As guard Cuttino Mobley said, "I love him. He's not a cocky kid. I just love playing with him." Yao was learning to joke around with them. Together, they had become a true team, a group that was growing together and getting better.

Incredibly, less than two months after many people were questioning whether he could make it in the NBA at all, Yao was expected to score twenty points or more every night, block a half dozen shots, and pull down ten or fifteen rebounds.

It wasn't realistic to think that he could do so all the time. Now that it was obvious that Yao could perform, most teams played him much closer than before, often double-teaming him to keep him away from the basket. The Rockets turned this to their advantage, however. As Coach Tomjanovich told his team when this happened, "Look into Yao, get them sucked in, swing it and get 'em on the weakside," which meant make the other team think that you are going to pass the ball to Yao, then throw it to an open man on the other side of the court. The young team learned fast. Yao continued to play well, and the Rockets continued to win.

In the meantime, Los Angeles Lakers center Shaquille O'Neal had returned to the lineup. After a slow start, the Lakers were beginning to hit their stride again.

Fans everywhere began to look ahead to the first meeting between the two big men, scheduled for January 17, 2003. The game would be televised nationally and in China. It was promoted with the hype of a boxing match — and included some speculation that the supposed animosity between Shaq and Yao went deeper than on-court rivalry.

A few weeks prior to the game, a clip of an interview that Shaquille O'Neal had given in June was played on the radio. In the interview, O'Neal was asked about Yao. In a mock Chinese accent he answered, "Tell Yao Ming 'Ching-chong-yang-wah-ah-soh.'" Shaq thought that those nonsense words sounded like Chinese.

Although O'Neal was trying to be funny, he offended many Chinese Americans, who felt that he was making fun of them and their culture. When the clip re-aired, reporters made sure that Yao heard O'Neal's comment and asked him if he was offended.

Yao impressed many observers with his mature and well-thought-out response. He wasn't angry with O'Neal, he said. "I believe Shaquille O'Neal was joking with what he said, but I think a lot of Asian people don't understand this joke."

He added that he didn't expect an apology from O'Neal, then made a joke at Shaq's expense, saying, "Chinese is hard to learn. Even when I was little, I took a long time to learn Chinese."

While hyping the game, the media tried to keep the controversy going, but neither O'Neal nor Yao was interested. O'Neal made a public apology a week prior to the game. Yao even tried to invite O'Neal to dinner, but O'Neal didn't get the invitation in time to accept.

The night of the game, Houston was buzzing. The match had been sold out for months, and scalpers were getting thousands of dollars for good seats. Before the game, two great former Rockets centers, Moses Malone and Hakeem Olajuwon, met with Yao, and the three had their picture taken together. Malone, who had helped teach Olajuwon the game, told Yao, "Don't back away from the challenge."

But not everyone thought that Yao and the Rockets

belonged on the same court with Shaq and the Lakers. Television analyst and former player Tom Tolbert said, "I've already penciled in Shaq for forty points. Yao is the new kid on the block, and Shaq is the best center in the game. . . . I think Shaq will say, 'Okay, you may be in first place in the All-Star voting, but let's make it clear who the best center in the game is.'"

At the start of the game, the two players met at mid-court for the opening tip off. Shaq leaned over to Yao and whispered something in his ear. Yao just smiled. Then the referee tossed the ball in the air, and the two went up together. The Lakers controlled the tap and moved the ball down the court.

O'Neal was confident. Although Yao was several inches taller, Shaq outweighed the Chinese center by at least seventy-five pounds, and he was much more experienced. He took position about fifteen feet away from the basket and called for the ball. When he caught the pass, he headed in and made a strong move to the basket.

But Yao was waiting. When O'Neal shot, the Rockets center swatted the ball away. The crowd erupted. O'Neal looked surprised. Yao quickly ran down the court.

Now it was the Rockets' turn. Eddie Griffin saw Yao down low and got him the ball. O'Neal leaned on Yao's back, but Yao spun and tossed in a hook shot over the shocked center for a basket.

The Rockets led, 2–0. The crowd was going crazy. As one Houston sports reporter wrote later, "The days of Shaq cruising unopposed, unchallenged by any big man, are over."

A few minutes later, Shaq tried to take another shot over Yao, and again Yao slapped it away. The Rockets took off on a fast break, and Yao finished the play by burying a turnaround jumper. Shaq tried to come right back at Yao, but for the third time in the quarter, Yao rejected one of Shaq's shots. For probably the first time in his career, Shaq wasn't necessarily the most intimidating player on the court. Never before had another NBA center made O'Neal look so bad.

Keyed by Yao's performance, the rest of the Rockets played one of their best games of the year. Steve Francis and Cuttino Mobley were deadly from the outside, and the team made the Lakers work hard for every shot.

Shaquille O'Neal, meanwhile, was forced to adjust to Yao. He finally started hitting his shots and slowly began wearing down the lighter man.

But Yao didn't give in. He kept Shaq busy and running, making it easier for the other Rockets to score.

However, with only eighteen seconds left, the Rockets trailed 92–89. Then they threw the ball inbounds to Yao. Yao looked around the court and took two quick dribbles, drawing the defense toward him. Steve Francis popped loose from a screen outside the three-point line. Yao made a perfect pass, and Francis drained the three pointer to tie the game.

The Lakers had thirteen seconds left to win. Star guard Kobe Bryant took the ball and probed the Houston defense. As the clock ticked down the final seconds, Bryant finally made his move, slashing to the basket. Over the years, Lakers fans had grown accustomed to watching Bryant take the winning shot in the final seconds of a game.

But Bryant hadn't had to contend with Yao Ming before. Yao left O'Neal and went out to meet Bryant, sticking his arm up to try to block the shot. The Lakers guard was forced to change his shot, and it bounced off the rim as time ran out. The game would enter overtime.

Once again, the two teams played each other evenly, trading shots. But with only a few seconds remaining in overtime, the Rockets had the ball and held a two-point lead.

Steve Francis had already poured in 44 points. He decided to take the ball at the Lakers once more. He drove down the lane toward the basket. Shaquille O'Neal, guarding Yao, had to make a quick decision to either challenge Francis or stay with Yao.

He chose to go after Francis. As he stepped out to block the guard's path to the basket, Yao stepped inside. Francis stopped and fired a bullet pass around Shaq to Yao.

Yao took the pass on the move and went straight to the hoop before a startled O'Neal had a chance to recover. Then Yao threw down a tremendous dunk to give the Rockets an insurmountable 108–104 lead.

The cheer of the Rockets fans echoed through the arena. Seconds later, the game ended. The Rockets had won!

The Houston players congratulated each other at midcourt as the Lakers trudged off to their locker room. Although O'Neal had finished the game with 31 points to Yao's 10, and O'Neal had out-rebounded Yao 13 to 10, there was no question that Yao's playing early in the game had set the tone for the Rockets, and his playing late in the game had sealed the win.

Yao was very happy after the game. "I have never faced a player like him before," he said. "It is every player's dream to play against the best center in America. That's life, that's the way the world is. You just have to face it. I feel like I was under water for a long time. Now I can finally breathe."

O'Neal was philosophical. He knew that the two would face each other many more times. "He plays big and he's a pretty good player," he said of Yao. "He's a nice guy."

Yao kept the game in perspective, too. "How should I put it? We beat the Lakers today," he said. "Shaq is still Shaq. One of the most positive things about America is everyone can fight for equality. But on the court, sometimes there is inequality. Shaq is bigger and stronger than everybody." But as Yao and the Rockets had proven, that didn't have to mean that Shaq's team was better.

Chapter Eleven:
2003

Worldwide All-Star

The win over the Lakers gave the Rockets a 23–15 record. With the season approaching the halfway point, it seemed as if the Rockets were on the precipice of becoming a playoff team. But the NBA season lasts a grueling 82 games. The season wasn't even halfway over.

Every NBA player has to adjust to the length of the season. It takes many players several years to adapt. The young Rockets still had to make that adjustment. Just when it appeared as if they were about to become one of the best teams in the league, they hit what players call "the wall" and ran out of energy.

Yao suddenly seemed to have lost a step. His scoring and rebounding average dropped. In some games, he almost disappeared again. Part of the reason was that as his teammates slumped, the opposition could guard him closer. But he was also exhausted.

He had been playing basketball almost non-stop for more than a year, moving from the CBA to the national team to the NBA without a break. In addition, he had had to adjust to a new country, a new culture, a new language, and the demands of suddenly becoming one of the most famous athletes in the world.

Coach Tomjanovich had been an All-Star player himself. He worked with Yao and tweaked the offense a little to take some of the pressure off his center. Instead of always throwing the ball inside at the beginning of the play, the Rockets now tried to finish inside, giving Yao a bit of a break.

Yao broke out of his slump with a big game against Dallas on January 29. It came at just the right time. The All-Star game was approaching, and Yao wanted to play well.

Yao had collected more votes than any other player and had been elected over the Lakers' Shaquille O'Neal to start the game at center. But he wasn't under any illusions that he was the best player in the league, or even the best center or the best player on his team. While Yao had played much better than anyone had expected, he knew that he still had a long way to go before he could be considered the equal of O'Neal or Tim Duncan. While he could occasionally outplay them, he knew that until he did so consistently, he would just be a young player with unknown potential.

Still, Yao was thrilled to travel to Atlanta for the All-Star game — and people were thrilled to have a chance to watch him play. Even people who didn't follow basketball closely knew who he was, in part because he had appeared in a commercial for a computer company. In the commercial, Yao sits in an airplane with a tiny laptop computer next to actor Vernon Troyer, who holds a much larger laptop. Even sitting down, Yao towers over Troyer, who is barely three feet tall. Yao doesn't say a word in the commercial — he doesn't have to. He just turns and looks down at Troyer and laughs. Now people who never watched basketball suddenly knew who Yao was. As a result, people who had never watched it before tuned into the All-Star game, just to see Yao.

He didn't disappoint anyone. Just one minute into the game, teammate Steve Francis lobbed a pass over the defense toward Yao, who was running hard down the court. Yao timed his catch perfectly, snagging the ball just short of the basket, then slamming into the basket in one sure, smooth move. The fans went nuts.

After his start, Yao played sparingly in the game, which is often the case for a rookie. He didn't care, though. He just enjoyed meeting many of the players whom he had once known only from television. He even got to spend some time with Shaquille O'Neal, who made certain to go over and introduce himself to Yao's parents, a gesture of respect appreciated by Yao. But because the game was the last All-Star-game appearance of the great Michael Jordan, Jordan was rightfully the focus of the day. Yao would have many more seasons to play in the All-Star game.

After the All-Star break, the Rockets took aim on earning a playoff berth. But first, they had to play the Lakers again. To the disappointment of many, Shaquille O'Neal missed the contest, this time because of a knee injury. Nevertheless, the game was a classic that went into double overtime. The Rockets and Lakers were developing quite a rivalry.

With Shaq out, Kobe Bryant took over and exploded for 52 points. Yao responded to lead the Rockets with 24 points. But he fouled out for the first time in his NBA career at the end of the first overtime period. Without Yao, the Rockets simply couldn't keep up. Los Angeles emerged with a 106–99 win.

In order to make the playoffs, the Rockets knew that they would have to perform well. Most of the best teams in the 2002–2003 NBA season seemed to be in the Western Division. Los Angeles, Sacramento, Dallas, and San Antonio all looked to have a chance at reaching the finals. The Rockets were one of five or six teams scrambling to earn one of the four remaining playoff spots.

But in mid-March, the Rockets were shaken when Coach Tomjanovich was diagnosed with bladder cancer and entered the hospital. Assistant coach Larry Smith took over. It was difficult for the team to retain its focus, and a tough schedule that put it on the road for much of the last month of the season didn't make its task any easier. And once again, Yao and several of his teammates had run out of steam and were trying to push through the wall.

There were other distractions as well. When the Rockets traveled to New Jersey at the beginning of April, NBA commissioner David Stern chose to hold a big meeting between Yao and other NBA officials to let Yao know just how big of an impact he had had on the NBA, particularly overseas. In China alone, as many as 300 million people were now watching Rockets games on television. Due to Yao Ming, nearly one quarter of the world's population was being introduced to NBA basketball.

Even Stern and other NBA officials were shocked by Yao's tremendous popularity. In only one short season, he had accomplished what they had hoped might happen over a decade or more. Stern thanked Yao for being so patient with the media and told him just how huge the NBA was becoming in China. "America is learning things about China, and a lot of people are learning about America through him," explained Stern. "That's the best we can do in sport.

It may be America's game, but it is captivating the world." And Yao Ming was basketball's greatest ambassador.

Yao came away from the meeting more fully aware of his importance and his responsibilities. But they did not overwhelm him. Yao even told Stern that in addition to winning an NBA championship, he wanted to win a gold medal for China in the 2008 Olympics. "I am a very greedy person," joked Yao.

Despite their best efforts, over the last few weeks of the season, the Rockets simply ran out of steam. Fatigue, worry about their coach, and a tough schedule combined to bump them from the playoffs despite a better-than-.500 record of 42–40.

Still, the Rockets had had a successful season. Team owner Leslie Anderson even announced that, while disappointed, "I love this team." He hoped that the playoffs, and even a world championship, would be in the club's future.

Yao was contemplative. When asked to describe the season, he responded, "I use an old Chinese expression: pain and happiness exist together." Although he was disappointed not to have made the playoffs and worried about the health of Coach

Tomjanovich, who would eventually have to resign to focus on his treatment, Yao was happy to have played so well. For the season, he averaged 13.5 points per game, with eight rebounds, nearly two blocked shots, and nearly two assists per game — good enough to finish second to Amare Stoudemire of Phoenix in Rookie of the Year voting.

Shortly after the end of the season, Yao returned home to Shanghai to fulfill his responsibilities with the Chinese national team. He was also called upon to use his international fame to help his country in a time of crisis.

Soon after Yao returned to China, the country was plagued by an outbreak of a mysterious and deadly disease known as severe acute respiratory syndrome, or SARS. The Chinese government had to tell its citizens what to do to help prevent the spread of the disease. Who better to spread the word than perhaps the most famous citizen of all, Yao Ming? As one reporter noted, "For China, he encompasses everything people want to be. He's larger than life, strong, intelligent, an international star, a family man, a team player." All these qualities made him the perfect candidate to serve as the host of a three-hour telethon and charity drive on Chinese television that raised millions of dollars to help SARS victims. During the "Stars vs. SARS" telethon, Yao explained how the disease spread and how people could avoid acquiring the disease. He may have helped save hundreds, even thousands of lives.

Yao Ming is a person who has already demonstrated that he has the ability to bring people from different nations and cultures together and foster greater understanding among all. He is only at the beginning of what promises to be an amazing career. Yet he continues to keep things in perspective. As he told one reporter, "All of the Chinese people say, 'Oh Yao Ming, you are all the Chinese hopes.' That's a lot of pressure. I'm just a basketball player."

With that kind of attitude, Yao Ming is sure to become much more than that.

Matt Christopher®

Lance Armstrong

Kobe Bryant

Jennifer Capriati

Terrell Davis

Julie Foudy

Jeff Gordon

Wayne Gretzky

Ken Griffey Jr.

Mia Hamm

Tony Hawk

Grant Hill

Ichiro

Derek Jeter

Randy Johnson

Michael Jordan

Mario Lemieux

Tara Lipinski

Mark McGwire

Greg Maddux

Hakeem Olajuwon

Shaquille O'Neal

Alex Rodriguez

Curt Schilling

Briana Scurry

Sammy Sosa

Venus and
Serena Williams

Tiger Woods

Steve Young

MATT CHRISTOPHER®

Read them all!

- Baseball Flyhawk
- Baseball Pals
- Baseball Turnaround
- The Basket Counts
- Body Check
- Catch That Pass!
- Catcher with a Glass Arm
- Center Court Sting
- Challenge at Second Base
- The Comeback Challenge
- Cool as Ice
- The Counterfeit Tackle
- The Diamond Champs
- Dirt Bike Racer
- Dirt Bike Runaway
- Dive Right In

- Double Play at Short
- Face-Off
- Fairway Phenom
- Football Fugitive
- Football Nightmare
- The Fox Steals Home
- Goalkeeper in Charge
- The Great Quarterback Switch
- Halfback Attack*
- The Hockey Machine
- Ice Magic
- Inline Skater
- Johnny Long Legs
- The Kid Who Only Hit Homers
- Long-Arm Quarterback
- Long Shot for Paul

*Originally published as *Crackerjack Halfback*

Look Who's Playing First Base

Miracle at the Plate

Mountain Bike Mania

No Arm in Left Field

Nothin' but Net

Olympic Dream

Penalty Shot

Pressure Play

Prime-Time Pitcher

Red-Hot Hightops

The Reluctant Pitcher

Return of the Home Run Kid

Roller Hockey Radicals

Run, Billy, Run

Run for It

Shoot for the Hoop

Shortstop from Tokyo

Skateboard Renegade

Skateboard Tough

Slam Dunk

Snowboard Champ

Snowboard Maverick

Snowboard Showdown

Soccer Duel

Soccer Halfback

Soccer Scoop

Spike It!

Stealing Home

Miracle at the Plate

Supercharged Infield

The Team That Couldn't Lose

Tennis Ace

Tight End

Too Hot to Handle

Top Wing

Touchdown for Tommy

Tough to Tackle

Wheel Wizards

Windmill Windup

Wingman on Ice

The Year Mom Won the Pennant

All available in paperback from Little, Brown and Company